Personality Test

"Let's find out your personality"

Instruction

1. You will see 4 sets of slide (A,B,C,D)
2. Each set - 19 Words
3. Give a score on the answer App

0 = not at all

1 = somewhat

2 = mostly

3 = very much

Name

( )　　( )　　( )　　( )

LION　　**OTTER**　　**GOLDEN RETREIVER**　　**BEAVER**

60
59
58
57
56
55
54
53
52
51
50
49
48
47
46
45
44
43
42
41
40
39
38
37
36
35
34
33
32
31
30
29
28
27
26
25
24
23
22
21
20
19
18
17
16
15
14
13
12
11
10
9
8
7
6
5
4
3
2
1
0

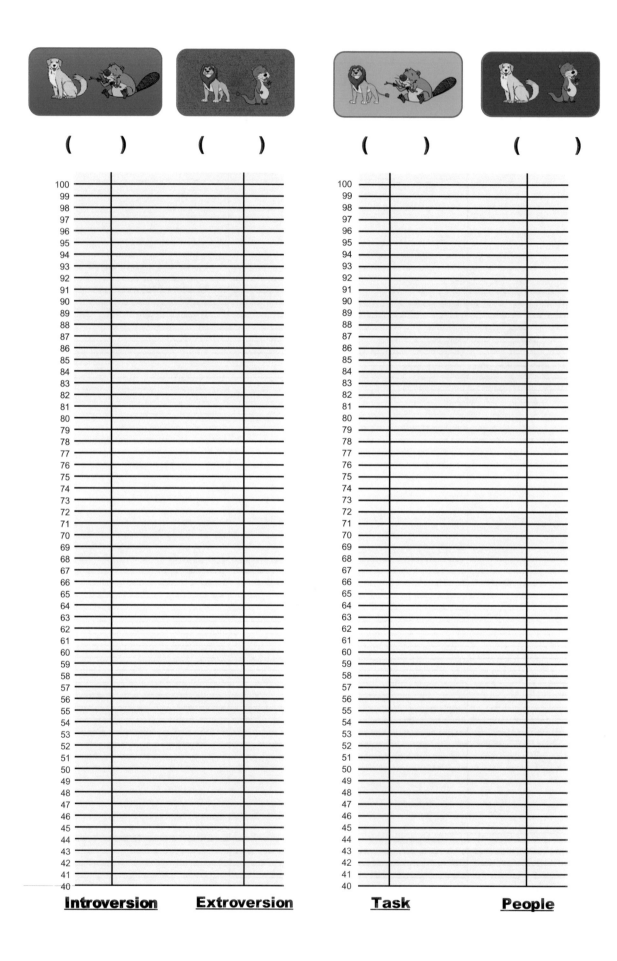

THE POINT

"Everyone
is
different"

GOALS

#1. **Underline: Understand** who you are
– Know yourself

#2. **Underline: Understand** who your people are
– Know your people.

"WE ARE DIFFERENT"

"Cross your arms"

Points

a. There is not a right or wrong

b. Don't judge. Understand and accept instead.

c. No one is the same as you.

KEY POINTS

- There are four different personalities.

- Lion, Otter, Golden Retriever and Beaver

- Everyone has four different personality types within them. However, each person has a dominant type. It's beneficial to understand yourself and others.

We are all different

It's important to understand that everyone is unique. People often see things from their own perspective, which can lead to misunderstandings. To prevent these issues, we need to embrace each other's differences. This helps us communicate better, solve problems, and collaborate more effectively. Imagine a workplace where everyone works harmoniously—that's how successful organizations thrive. Great leaders are effective communicators.

"Communication is the real work of leadership." - Nitin Nohria.

To be a great leader, you need strong communication skills. By understanding different personality types, you can become an even more effective communicator.

WHEN YOU GO TO HOSPITAL...

- How is your pain?
- How is your pain level?

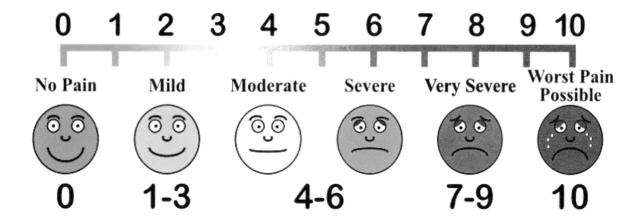

WHAT IS YOUR PERSONALITY?

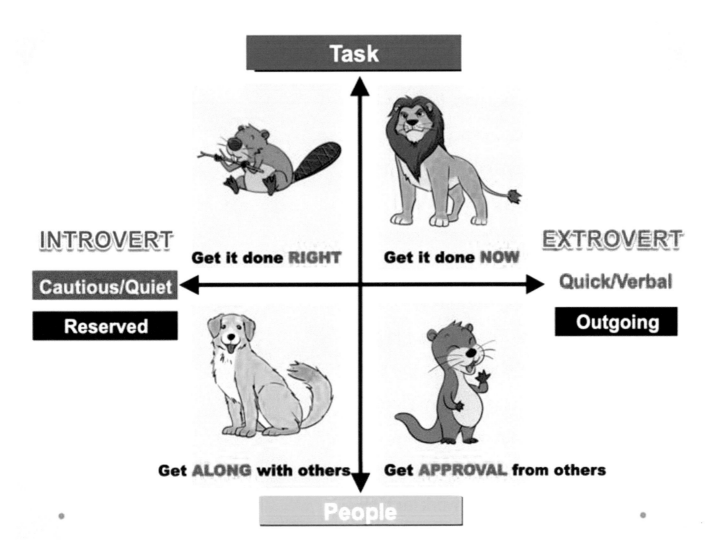

Introverts VS Extroverts

Carl Jung, a Swiss psychiatrist, introduced the concepts of introversion and extraversion. Introverts focus on their internal thoughts and feelings, finding energy in solitude and preferring low-stimulus environments. They are often reserved and introspective. Extraverts, in contrast, are energized by social interactions and thrive in high-stimulus environments. They are outgoing, sociable, and enjoy being the center of attention. Jung's theory suggests these traits exist on a continuum, with individuals exhibiting varying degrees of both. His work laid the foundation for modern personality psychology and influenced assessments like the Myers-Briggs Type Indicator

Carl Jung

Introverts VS Extroverts

Introverts	Extroverts
• A good listener	• Speak before thinking
• Friend group consists of a few very close people	• Feel an energy boost from social situations
• You are sought out by many for your words of wisdom	• Don't like to be alone
• Don't like to talk with strangers	• If there is a problem, you prefer to talk it.
• People ask why you are so quiet	• Your friend group is very large, but the connections are not super close
• Feel that working individually is better than working in groups	

LION

DOMINANT

D DOMINANT

D TYPES ARE	D TYPES DON'T LIKE
Quick to respond	Indecision
Goal oriented	Slow people
Performance conscious	Talkers who don't produce
Hard to please	Lazy people
Self Confident	Details
Industrious	Taking orders
Firm	

Understanding & Valuing

Major strengths

Gets things done

Decisive

Persistent

Initiates change

Major weaknesses

Insensitive to others

Impatient (overlooks risks and facts)

Stubborn and unyielding

WHEN UNDER PRESSURE

- Raise their voice

- Become challenging and may bully others

- Behave arrogantly

WHEN UNDER PRESSURE

- They are assertive and excel at expressing their viewpoints. They tend to have a low tolerance for correction and differing opinions.

- Extreme Lion behavior may go into 'attack mode' when obstacles arise. They become angry and frustrated due to a sense of losing control. This reaction is not personal; you just happen to be in their line of fire.

If you have a Lion Type Boss...

DON'T:

- Don't be neutral.

- They detest wishy-washy

- Don't be unprepared.

- Excuses

DO:

- Do stick to the point.

- Do speak business-like.

- Know your stuff!!!

- Take a stand for black or white.

OTTER

INSPIRING

I INSPIRING

I TYPES ARE	I TYPES DON'T LIKE
Fun to watch	Being ignored
Great starters	Being isolated
Poor finishers	Being ridiculed
Likeable	Repetitive tasks
Prone to exaggerate	Detail work
Easily excitable	

Understanding & Valuing

Major strengths

Optimistic
Personable
Enthusiastic
Inspirational

Major weaknesses

Impulsive
Verbally manipulative
Lacks follow-through

WHEN UNDER PRESSURE

- **Talk loudly and quickly**

- **Disorganized and scatterbrained**

If you have a Otter Type Boss...

DON'T:

- Don't give them too many details

- Don't try and conform them to rigid thinking

- Don't make the feel unappreciated

DO:

- Do be flexible

- Do illustrations and demonstrations

- Do let them talk

- Do persuade them with enthusiasm

GOLDEN RETRIEVER

SUPPORTIVE

S SUPPORTIVE

S TYPES ARE	S TYPES DON'T LIKE
Sweetest people	Insensitivity
Easily manipulated	To be yelled at
Loyal friends	Misunderstandings
Team players	Sarcasm
Poor starters	Surprises
Great finishers	Being pushed

Understanding & Valuing

Major strengths	**Major weaknesses**
Supportive	Indirect with others
Agreeable	Resists quick
Loyal	change
Values relationships	Overly tolerant

WHEN UNDER PRESSURE

- Submit

- Accommodate

- Agree with Everybody

- These people often take on too much and don't deliver on what they promised.

- Because they have a strong desire to please and get along with others, they find it difficult to say 'no'.

If you have a Golden Retrievers Type Boss...

DON'T:

- Don't ignore their feelings.

- Don't be too formal or intense.

- Don't be rude.

DO:

- Do encourage them to make decisions.

- Do encourage their honest opinions.

- Do slow down and listen to them.

- Do reassure them.

BEAVER

CAUTIOUS

C CAUTIOUS

C TYPES ARE	C TYPES DON'T LIKE
Perfectionists	Being criticized
Difficult to satisfy	Mistakes
Logical	Sudden changes
Meticulous	Shoddy work
Self-sacrificing	Un-preparedness
Inquisitive	Interruptions

Understanding & Valuing

Major strengths

Orderly
Thorough
Analytical
Pursues excellence

Major weaknesses

Lacks spontaneity
Critical
Overly cautious

WHEN UNDER PRESSURE

- Become silent

- Flee or withdraw

- Exhibit negative behavior

- They may become chronic complainers if something isn't 'right' and they don't know how to fix it.

- They usually have a large workload and may not know how to delegate.

- They have great difficulty making snap decisions

If you have a Beaver Type Boss...

DON'T:

- Don't be inconsistent

- Don't lose your temper with them; they will close down and not communicate.

DO:

- Do be factual, logical and structured

- Do schedule time to meet; they don't like being caught off guard

PERSONALITIES INTERPRETATION

LION

DOMINANT

Lion

Let's talk about your primary personality, which is "Lion."

Basic Tendencies: You're fast-paced and task-oriented. You thrive on action and getting things done efficiently.

Greatest Strengths: Your decisive action and ability to take charge help you get results. You're self-confident, independent, and not afraid to take risks.

Natural Limitations: Sometimes, you might feel restless or impatient. You can be stubborn and blunt, which might come across as too direct to others.

Communication: You tend to communicate in a one-way, direct manner, focusing on the bottom line. You value clear, straightforward conversations.

Fears: Your biggest fears include losing control, being taken advantage of, and being scrutinized too closely.

Under Pressure: When under pressure, you might become autocratic, aggressive, and demanding. You like to take charge and ensure things get done.

Work Style: At work, you're critical, blunt, and forceful. You're direct in your approach, good at delegating, and always focused on getting things done. You also question the status quo, always looking for better ways to achieve results.

Decision Making: You make quick, result-focused decisions. You don't like to waste time and prefer to act swiftly.

Greatest Needs: You need challenges, change, and choices. Direct answers are important to you, and you could benefit from more empathy in interactions.

Wants: You seek new and varied activities, credit for your accomplishments, power, and a leading position. You like to be the first and enjoy recognition.

Recovery: To recharge, you prefer engaging in physical activities.

Orientation: You're results-oriented. You shape your environment by overcoming opposition, always striving to achieve your goals.

Understanding these aspects of your personality can help you leverage your strengths and address your limitations, leading to more effective communication and personal growth.

The Lion's Strengths and Weaknesses

At Emotions

Let's start with your emotions. As a Lion, you naturally embody leadership. You're dynamic and active, always ready to take charge and correct any wrongs you see. Your strong will and decisiveness set you apart, and you approach situations without letting emotions cloud your judgment. You're not easily discouraged, showcasing an impressive level of independence and self-sufficiency. Your confidence is palpable, and you have the capability to run almost anything effectively.

However, with these strengths come a few weaknesses. You can be bossy and impatient, quick to temper and unable to relax. Your impetuous nature might lead you to enjoy controversy and arguments more than most. Even when losing, you have a hard time giving up. You might come across too strong, inflexible, and not complimentary enough. Tears and emotions aren't something you deal well with, and you can appear unsympathetic at times.

At Work

In the workplace, your strengths truly shine. You're incredibly goal-oriented and have a knack for seeing the whole picture. Organizing and seeking practical solutions come naturally to you. You move quickly to action, delegate work efficiently, and ensure that goals are met. Your ability to stimulate activity and thrive on opposition keeps your work environment dynamic and productive.

But there are weaknesses to be mindful of. You have little tolerance for mistakes and often don't bother with analyzing details, finding trivia boring. This can lead you to make rash decisions. Sometimes, you might come off as rude or tactless, and you have a tendency to manipulate people to achieve your goals. Your demanding nature means you expect a lot from others, and you might believe that the end justifies the means. Work can become your central focus, almost like a god, and you demand loyalty from those around you.

Understanding these strengths and weaknesses can help you harness your natural abilities while addressing areas for improvement, leading to a more balanced and effective approach in both personal and professional settings.

OTTER

INSPIRING

Otter

Let's talk about your primary personality, which is "Otter."

Basic Tendencies: You're fast-paced and people-oriented. You thrive in social settings and love being around others.

Greatest Strengths: You're fun-loving, always involved, and bring enthusiasm to everything you do. Your emotional and optimistic nature makes you a great communicator, able to inspire and connect with people easily.

Natural Limitations: Sometimes, you might find yourself disorganized and not detail-oriented. Your optimistic outlook can also make you a bit unrealistic at times.

Communication: You communicate in a positive, inspiring, and persuasive manner. Your words often lift others and motivate them to join in your enthusiasm.

Fears: You fear being in a fixed environment, losing social approval, and having your time closely audited. You thrive on flexibility and social interaction.

Under Pressure: When under pressure, you might attack but often avoid public confrontation. Your approach is to manage stress without causing a scene.

Work Style: At work, you're persuasive and mobile, bringing energy and friendliness to your tasks. You inspire others and maintain an "open door" policy, making you approachable and easy to work with.

Decision Making: You tend to make impulsive decisions based on whether something "feels" right. Your intuition guides you more than meticulous planning.

Greatest Needs: You need better control of your time, fun activities, social recognition, freedom from dealing with details, and a more objective outlook.

Wants: You want to be convincing, work in a favorable environment, and gain social approval. These elements help you feel fulfilled and motivated.

Recovery: To recharge, you seek out social time. Being around others helps you regain your energy and enthusiasm.

Orientation: You shape your environment by working through people. Your ability to connect and inspire allows you to influence and bring about positive change in your surroundings.

Understanding these aspects of your personality can help you leverage your strengths and address your limitations, leading to more effective communication and personal growth.

The Otter's Strengths and Weaknesses

At Emotions

When it comes to your emotions, as an Otter, you have an appealing personality that's hard to resist. You're naturally talkative and a great storyteller, often becoming the life of the party. Your sense of humor is sharp, and you have a knack for remembering colorful details. You engage physically with your listeners, are very emotional and demonstrative, and your cheerfulness is infectious. You're curious, good on stage, and often appear wide-eyed and innocent, living in the moment with a changeable disposition. At heart, you're sincere and maintain a childlike wonder.

However, there are a few weaknesses to be aware of. You can be a compulsive talker, sometimes exaggerating and elaborating on stories. You might dwell on trivial matters and have trouble remembering names, which can scare others off. Your boundless happiness can be overwhelming for some, and your restless energy might come across as egotistical. At times, you might bluster and complain, appear naive, and have a loud voice and laugh. You can be controlled by circumstances, get angry easily, seem phony to some, and maintain a childlike demeanor.

At Work

In the workplace, your strengths shine through. You're quick to volunteer for jobs and are full of new ideas for activities. You present yourself well, with a creative and colorful approach that brings energy and enthusiasm to your tasks. You start projects in a flashy way, inspiring and charming others to join in and contribute.

On the flip side, you sometimes prefer talking over working, which can lead to forgotten obligations and a lack of follow-through. Your confidence might fade quickly, and you can be undisciplined with priorities often out of order. Decisions are made based on feelings, and you can be easily distracted, wasting time with excessive talking.

Understanding these strengths and weaknesses can help you harness your natural abilities while addressing areas for improvement, leading to a more balanced and effective approach in both personal and professional settings.

GOLDEN RETRIEVER

SUPPORTIVE

Golden Retriever

Let's talk about your primary personality, which is "Golden Retriever."

Basic Tendencies: You're slow-paced and people-oriented. You take your time to connect deeply with those around you, fostering strong relationships.

Greatest Strengths: Your patience is remarkable, and you're easy-going, making you a fantastic team player. You bring a calming influence to any situation and offer stability. Your systematic approach helps keep things in order.

Natural Limitations: Sometimes, you might find yourself indecisive and over-accommodating, being too passive when you need to be assertive.

Communication: You're a two-way communicator and the best listener. You provide empathetic feedback, making others feel heard and understood.

Fears: You fear losing financial or emotional security and dislike sudden changes. Stability is very important to you.

Under Pressure: When under pressure, you tend to acquiesce, tolerate, and comply to keep the peace.

Work Style: At work, you're patient and traditional, preferring a team-oriented approach. You're a specialist in your field, contributing steadily and reliably.

Decision Making: Your decision-making is relational, relying on trust in others. You value the input and feelings of those around you.

Greatest Needs: You need the status quo and security. You require time to adjust to change, a conflict-free environment, and order and sequence in your tasks.

Wants: You seek your family's approval, demonstrated sincerity from others, reassurance, and appreciation for your efforts.

Recovery: To recharge, you need "nothing time" – periods where you can relax without any demands or distractions.

Orientation: You focus on projects, doing your part and cooperating with others to get the job done. Your collaborative nature helps create a cohesive and effective team.

Understanding these aspects of your personality can help you leverage your strengths and address your limitations, leading to more effective communication and personal growth.

The Golden Retriever's Strengths and Weaknesses

At Emotions

As a Golden Retriever, your emotional strengths are quite distinctive. You have a low-key personality and are easy-going and relaxed. You're calm, cool, and collected, which makes you patient and well-balanced. Your consistent demeanor brings stability to those around you. Though quiet, you possess a witty sense of humor. You're sympathetic and kind, often keeping your emotions hidden. You are happily reconciled to life and can adapt to various situations, making you an all-purpose person.

However, there are a few emotional weaknesses to note. You might come across as unenthusiastic at times and can be fearful and worried. Indecisiveness is a challenge, and you may avoid taking on responsibilities. Despite your quiet nature, you have a quiet will of iron, which can sometimes be seen as stubbornness. You might be perceived as selfish or too shy and reticent. Additionally, you tend to compromise too much and can appear self-righteous.

At Work

In the workplace, your strengths are invaluable. You're competent and steady, bringing a peaceful and agreeable presence. You have strong administrative abilities and excel at mediating problems, often avoiding conflicts. You're good under pressure and adept at finding the easy way to get things done.

On the flip side, your work-related weaknesses include not being very goal-oriented and lacking self-motivation. It can be hard to get you moving, and you may resent being pushed. At times, you might be lazy and careless, which can discourage others around you. You tend to prefer watching rather than actively participating.

Recognizing these strengths and weaknesses can help you understand your natural tendencies better and find ways to enhance your effectiveness both emotionally and professionally.

BEAVER

CAUTIOUS

Beaver

Let's talk about your primary personality, which is "Beaver."

Basic Tendencies: You're slow-paced and task-oriented, taking your time to ensure everything is done correctly and thoroughly.

Greatest Strengths: Your accuracy and analytical skills are impressive. You pay attention to detail and hold high standards. Your intuition and controlled demeanor help you navigate complex tasks effectively.

Natural Limitations: Sometimes, you can be too critical and perfectionistic, which may lead to being overly sensitive to criticism or mistakes.

Communication: You communicate diplomatically, are a good listener, and always provide detailed information. This makes your communication clear and effective.

Fears: You fear criticism of your work or performance and making mistakes. These fears can drive you to strive for perfection.

Under Pressure: When under pressure, you tend to avoid confrontation, ignore distractions, and plan a strategy to address the issue.

Work Style: Your work style is characterized by accuracy, caution, and a critical eye. You strive for perfection in every task you undertake.

Decision Making: You can be reluctant to make decisions without having all the necessary information. You prefer to have a lot of data before making a choice.

Greatest Needs: You need defined responsibilities and sufficient time to complete tasks with quality. Personal support, no surprises, and appreciation for your work are essential for you to thrive.

Wants: You prefer limited exposure and value quality, privacy, and accuracy in everything you do.

Recovery: To recharge, you need private time to reflect and unwind.

Orientation: You focus on tasks, working within existing circumstances to promote quality and service.

Understanding these aspects of your personality can help you leverage your strengths and address your limitations, leading to more effective communication and personal growth.

The Beaver's Strengths and Weaknesses

At Emotions

When it comes to your emotions, you have many strengths. You are deep and thoughtful, always analyzing situations from multiple angles. You take things seriously and approach life with a sense of purpose. Your talents are vast, often manifesting in creative or artistic abilities, and you have a natural inclination towards music and the arts. You're philosophical and poetic, with a deep appreciation for beauty in the world around you. Sensitivity to others' feelings and a self-sacrificing nature make you conscientious and idealistic, always striving to do what's right and just.

However, these strengths come with their own set of challenges. You tend to remember negative experiences, which can lead to moodiness and depression. Sometimes, you might even seem to enjoy being hurt, perhaps as a way to validate your deep emotions. This can be tied to a sense of false humility and a tendency to escape into your own world. Your low self-image and selective hearing can make you seem self-centered and too introspective. Feelings of guilt and a persecution complex can also weigh heavily on you, and you might even lean towards hypochondria, worrying excessively about your health.

At Work

In the workplace, your strengths shine brightly. You are quick to volunteer for jobs and think up new activities, always bringing fresh ideas to the table. Your creative and colorful approach makes everything you do look great on the surface. You bring energy and enthusiasm to your work, starting projects with a flashy, inspiring zeal that motivates others to join in. Your charm helps you rally others to work alongside you.

However, your focus on tasks rather than people can sometimes be a weakness. You might get depressed over imperfections and choose difficult work that others might avoid. Hesitancy to start projects and spending too much time planning can slow you down. You often prefer analysis over actual work, which can make you hard to please. Your standards are often too high, leading to self-deprecation and a deep need for approval from others. This constant search for validation can be exhausting and make you feel like you're never quite good enough.

Understanding these aspects of your personality can help you harness your strengths and address your weaknesses, leading to a more balanced and fulfilling life.

Feed Back

LION

DOMINANT

How was this TNG?

- Was it Good?
- Did you learn something from this TNG?

OTTER

INSPIRING

How was this TNG?

- **Was it Fun?**
- **Did you have fun?**

GOLDEN RETRIEVER

SUPPORTIVE

How was this TNG?

What are your feeling about this Training?

BEAVER

CAUTIOUS

How was this TNG?

Rate this Training?

(1=least, 5=Outstanding)

Instructor   (1,2,3,4,5)

Contents   (1,2,3,4,5)

Usefulness   (1,2,3,4,5)

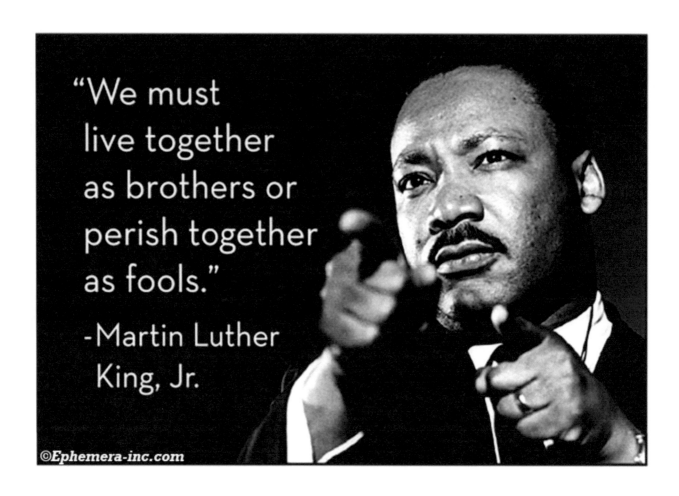

"We must live together as brothers or perish together as fools."

-Martin Luther King, Jr.

©Ephemera-inc.com

Made in United States
Troutdale, OR
12/03/2024

25767579R00040